Presented To

By

Forget-me-not
Timeless Sentiments for Lifelong Friends
© 2002 by Janda Sims Kelley

published by Multnomah Publishers, Inc.
P.O. Box 1720, Sisters, OR 97759

ISBN 1-57673-933-3

Designed by Koechel Peterson & Associates, Minneapolis, MN

Multnomah Publishers, Inc. has made every effort to trace the ownership of all
poems and quotes. In the event of a question arising from the use of a poem or quote,
we regret any error made and will be pleased to make the necessary correction in
future editions of this book.

Scripture quotations are taken from *The Holy Bible*,
New International Version © 1973, 1984 by International Bible Society,
used by permission of Zondervan Publishing House; *The Living Bible* © (TLB)
1971, used by permission of Tyndale House Publishers, Inc.
All rights reserved.

*Multnomah* is a trademark of Multnomah Publishers, Inc., and is registered in the
U.S. Patent and Trademark Office.
The colophone is a trademark of Multnomah Publishers, Inc.

Printed in China

02 03 04 05 06 07 08 — 10 9 8 7 6 5 4 3 2 1 0

www.multnomahgifts.com

# Forget-me-&not

## Timeless Sentiments
## For Lifelong Friends

Written by

Janda Sims Kelley

# TABLE OF CONTENTS
## DEDICATION
## INTRODUCTION

# DEDICATION

This book is dedicated to my heavenly
Father, who has given me eternal life
filled with His grace; to my father,
Claude Sims, who showed me a godly life
by example; to my husband, Steve, who
richly blesses my life with love; and to my
sons, Stephen and Chad, who honor my
life with that beautiful name mother.
Thank you also to the wonderful
women and my cherished sisters in
Christ, who have prayed for me, loved
me, and encouraged me. You have made
me blessed among women.

# INTRODUCTION

I love treasure hunts. I really do. The thrill of looking and the excitement of finding always make my heart race. And in the pursuit of treasures, I've come to discover that sometimes treasures come in the most unusual of forms. It may be a piece of sterling hidden among stainless or a beautiful silk handkerchief buried in the linens—a treasure within a treasure. And treasure within a treasure is what I discovered in my first sentiment album.

I saw it lying on a dusty shelf in a quaint antique shop in North Carolina. The Aldine Album, addressed to Thena in 1885, was filled with hand-penned poems, etchings, sentiments, and autographs. Colorful floral stickers, calling cards, and pressed flowers graced the pages. Impressed first by their beauty, I then became fascinated with the grace and sincerity expressed in these time-worn pages. The messages from history, written and hidden in these albums so many years before, became fresh again as they spoke to my heart. I paused to think about the writer whose hand had diligently recorded these inspiring sentiments and thought about how amazed she would be to know that her words were touching another heart more than one hundred years later. These messages of eternal truth transcended the passing of time, speaking with charm and relevance of love, family, faith, and true friendship—matters most important in my life today. These sacred memories from bygone years revealed to me that, although times have changed, the desires and longings of women have remained the same. Today's more sophisticated lifestyle does not satisfy the deep, emotional

*To Bessie,*

*Life is a volume from youth to old age,*
*Each year finishes a chapter,*
　　*each day a page.*
*May none be more honored,*
　　*more womanly true,*
*Than that sketched yearly and daily by you.*

　*From Your Friend and Teacher,*
　*Sarah Brittenham*
　*November 19, 1900*

needs that God has planted in the feminine heart.

As I read each page, now yellowing with age, I felt a kinship with the women whose names were inscribed by their own hand. And though they are no longer walking life's path, their words remain a legacy of wisdom passed on to future generations. As time moves forward, their names will not be remembered, but the truth they imparted in those albums will endure. I feel blessed to have stepped into these women's lives and to have drawn priceless truths from their hearts. I claim no ownership of these endearing albums, for they have only been entrusted to me for safekeeping that I might share them with you. It is my desire that you find new strength and hope in these timeless messages.

My collection of albums continues to grow. I now have more than one hundred. Still, I can't resist purchasing another one in hopes that a treasured piece of wisdom may lie between its covers. Locks of hair, graduation and wedding announcements, genealogies, silk ribbons, Scripture verses, and colorful sketches are always a surprise. These little pieces of history have become friends to me, providing comfort in times of need and inspiration in times of discouragement.

As I read through each album, it became apparent to me that woven throughout the pages was a common thread—the beautiful sentiment "Forget-Me-Not." Through the art of remembrance, each page whispered devotion, sincerity, and faithfulness to lifelong friendships. And though the authors asked to not be forgotten, it is the words they wrote which should never be forsaken.

On my most recent treasure hunt I was attracted to some charming forget-me-nots that adorned the cover of an old book containing a simple poem by William Channing. I soon realized that its lines, which complemented the albums so well, offered the perfect theme for this book. Each line, a treasure in itself, serves as the subtitle for a chapter. I hope that you will sit with a cup of tea in a quiet place and let these messages from the past encourage you. My prayer is that these sentiments will help you focus on the timeless values that are precious treasures for our hurried lives. I invite you to join me as we peek into the past and hear from the gracious women who have gone before us... that we forget them not and that we glean a harvest among the many treasures they have left behind.

## MY SYMPHONY

TO LIVE CONTENT WITH SMALL MEANS.
TO SEEK ELEGANCE RATHER THAN
LUXURY, REFINEMENT
RATHER THAN FASHION.
TO BE WORTHY, NOT RESPECTABLE,
AND WEALTHY, NOT RICH.
TO STUDY HARD, THINK QUIETLY,
TALK GENTLY, AND ACT FRANKLY.
TO LISTEN TO STARS AND BIRDS,
TO BABES AND SAGES
WITH OPEN HEART.
TO BEAR ALL CHEERFULLY, DO ALL
BRAVELY, AWAIT OCCASIONS,
HURRY NEVER.
TO LET THE SPIRITUAL UNBIDDEN
AND UNCONSCIOUS GROW UP
THROUGH THE COMMON.
THIS IS TO BE MY SYMPHONY.

WILLIAM CHANNING

POST CARD.

S SIDE FOR CORRESPONDENCE · THE ADDRESS

## POST CARD

To Gracie,

Remember me, my dearest friend.

Remember me unto the end.

May every blessing be thy lot.

I'll only ask forget-me-not.

From Carrie, 1883.

em-ber me.

soon. Regards to Mr. Harper, Mamie, Mr. B.
and all the friends. Fan.

# CHAPTER ONE
## FINDING CONTENTMENT, KNOWING JOY
### To Live Content with Small Means

When I married my husband almost thirty years ago, I moved away from home to begin (I thought) a life in paradise. I knew that we are to be content in whatever state we're in, but I had no idea that would mean the kind of circumstances I found myself in! After several years, I convinced myself that I had taken a wrong turn and had slowly lost my way. Surely this was not the paradise I had dreamed about. I had expected a perfect life in every way, so I set out to find it and buy it. But as I filled my days with activities and my closets with things, I was filling my heart with bitterness and frustration, crowding it with unreasonable desires and great expectations. With a heart so full of pain, I knew no peace.

After years of struggling, I finally began to understand that contentment is an attitude of the heart. It cannot depend on circumstances, wealth, success, or other people. I also learned that I couldn't ease my aching heart with an overflowing shopping bag. I had to empty my heart—empty myself of myself—before I could be filled with the blessed gift of contentment.

So setting out on a path toward a change of heart, I chose to let go of the expectations and desires I had clutched so tightly. In their place, I planted seeds of gratitude. Each day,

To Mary,
Some friends may wish thee happiness,
Others may wish thee wealth
My wish for thee is better far
Contentment blest with health.

From Your Friend, Helen
Minnesota, September 5, 1895

# Forget-me-not

To Gracie,

Think of me when you are happy,

Keep for me one little spot.

In the depth of thine affection,

Plant a sweet forget-me-not.

Your True Friend, Mamie Goodwin
East Rochester, New Hampshire, January 11, 1888

instead of desiring more, I searched for the blessings around me that I had failed to see. I was amazed by the wealth of family, friends, and surroundings that I had not appreciated when my focus had been on my own wants. I also noticed that my search for contentment in all the wrong places had not only made me miserable, but had also stolen joy from those who loved me the most. A new attitude of thanksgiving permeated my heart when I replaced my grumbling with praise. I learned that giving thanks for small blessings left no room

for desires that would never satisfy or be fully satisfied. I realized that if I could not be content with what I had been given, I would never be content with what I wanted even if I received it. Contentment became the treasure that I could afford but could never buy.

Even though my heart has been changing, I have to renew my decision to choose gratitude every single day. There are still days when my contentment takes a vacation, but then I know that it was I who departed from it and not it from me. Sometimes I just don't feel like being thankful, but then I'm reminded of the joy that comes with all-inclusive gratitude, with being thankful for everything. Being content is a tough assignment in a busy world crowded with temptations—but it's well worth the effort, for it is filling my heart with joy.

Earlier, when I thought about this journey of life, I realized that I can walk it in victory or in defeat. By placing my feet on the path of thankfulness and peace, and by using the time, talents, and blessings that God has given me, I've found new opportunities for growth. The old desires that once so consumed me have melted away. My restless heart has found fulfillment in the smallest details of my life. Now I look for each blessing that has been prepared just for me, and I celebrate it. I rejoice in the beauty of my surroundings, my priceless friendships, my opportunities for service, a faithful church, the talents I have been given, and my special family. These are the richest blessings—appreciated even more thanks to the greatest grace of all, being content in all things. For I have been given sufficient provision for each new day—and that is enough for me.

*To Annie,*

*Of what are all*

*the joys we hold*

*compared to joys above us?*

*And what are rank,*

*power, and gold*

*compared to hearts*

*that love us?*

From Mallory, July 29, 1889

Forget

Forget-
me-not

I know what it is to be in need,
and I know what it is to have plenty.
I have learned the secret of being
content in any and every situation,
whether well fed or hungry,
whether living in plenty or in want.

Philippians 4:12–13

# Chapter Two

## Appreciating Inner Beauty

### To Seek Elegance Rather than Luxury

If there could be a heaven on earth, mine would be a large flea market full of hidden treasures. All day I could walk beside long tables covered with colorful glass, charming linens, and interesting memorabilia—and my feet would never get blisters!

Leave me at a flea market, and I lose track of time and reality. Row after row of stuff beckons me. I'm learning to pace myself and merely scan each table so I won't be overwhelmed. I'm training my eye to search for the elegant, to find the simple treasure among the random mix. Sometimes I have to stretch my imagination to find beauty in some of the more curious pieces. I wonder how often I've passed by hidden beauty, mistaking something for junk.

Now put on your walking shoes, and join me on a quick trip to the flea market to see what we can find.

Right away we spot two pieces of silver sitting side by side. One is highly polished and beautifully engraved; the other is unpolished and simply designed. I pick up both pieces, but I lay down the unpolished one. It doesn't appeal to my eye, and I decide it isn't worth the time to polish. In my haste I have passed by the more valuable and opted instead for the more immediately attractive.

You pick up what I have put down, for you see what I too quickly dismissed. Had I taken the time to consider the true value of the pieces, I would have discovered that my choice, though beautiful on the outside, was damaged on the inside. But your selection, with an outer beauty not readily apparent, proved to be sterling under the tarnish. The value of the two pieces could be determined only by considering their hidden traits. Presuming it to be more valuable, I

*Birthday Greeting*

To Bertha,

Within the

roughest shell uncouth

purest pearl may hide.

You'll often find

a heart of truth,

within a rough outside.

From Your Sister, Mary
Silver Springs, Maryland, 1883

*Forget-me-not*

TO GRACIE.

IF WATER SHOULD BETWEEN US ROLL,

AND DISTANT BE OUR LOT.

FOR FRIENDSHIPS SAKE, IF NOT FOR LOVE,

MY FRIEND, FORGET-ME-NOT.

Flora Shafer
Plymouth, Indiana, March 25, 1880

chose the fancier piece because it was visually appealing. But the value of the inside is what determines real worth.

How many times have I been so blinded by the beauty of the external that I missed the true value of the internal?

I confess that many times I, critical by nature, judge people by their outside appearance. I pay more attention to what my eyes see than to their hearts. Each time I do this, God humbles me through the grace that is shown to me by the very ones I had so quickly dismissed.

I live in a cosmopolitan community. People of different nationalities live side by side and work together. I'm ashamed to say that sometimes my first nature is to dismiss those whose traditions and languages are different from my own. It is all too easy for me to look only at the outside and assume that those differences should keep us apart. But when I make an effort to know the inside of a person, to know his or her heart, I am always amazed at the beauty I find. The goodness

found in that polished heart only magnifies the need for a good polishing of my own heart.

Just as with silver, we can remove the tarnish from our outside and still never reveal the crack on the inside. I can disguise my flaws with polish and decoration in an attempt to be as attractive as the flea market silver. After all, man can only see the outside—but God sees deeply into the heart. I rejoice and give thanks for the peace that comes with knowing that the One who sees my heart stands ready to polish and repair.

The LORD does not look
at the things man looks at.
Man looks at the outward appearance,
but the LORD looks at the heart.

1 Samuel 16:7

oral Album

To Alexandria,
The external form
may win the eye,
But the internal graces
should win the heart.

*From Freeman, 1883*

Greetings
and all good Wishes

A Happy
Birthday.

To Alice,
Charms strike the sight,
but merit
wins the soul.

*Your Teacher, Susie C. Beck.*
*Millersville, Pennsylvania*
*January 25, 1883*

# CHAPTER THREE

## CHOOSING THE GENUINE

### To Seek Refinement Rather than Fashion

Some of my favorite childhood memories center around a big box of dress-up clothes. Inside that brightly colored treasure chest were Mom's dresses, shoes, hats, and jewelry—the gateway to countless hours in a make-believe world. In just an hour, I could be a princess, a teacher, and a mother. I could be anybody I wanted to be simply by putting on someone else's clothes. My love for clothes and fashion started with that box. My husband will tell you that my passion continues today: He has one closet. I have the rest.

Although I no longer play dress-up, I often remember Mom's dress-up box. But now that I think about it, nothing really fit, and I only felt better for a little while. I suppose I had to get used to my own clothes, my own roles.

Styles change so quickly that the day after you have purchased the latest, it can suddenly prove to be passé.

Trying to stay in vogue is a lesson in futility! Yet it's amazing how often we choose that course. Models dressed in sleek new clothes suggest what we should be. Some of us follow the world's design, believing that doing so will make us happier or more acceptable or more admired or more respected or, or, or. We try to make someone else's style our own, even when there's no fit at all. Just because a designer says something is fashionable doesn't mean we should be wearing it. Does it?

If you're like me, most modern fashions are completely off limits. I feel more comfortable wearing certain styles and colors because I know they fit who I am and the kind of life I lead. I feel more confident when I wear clothing that I choose to suit my style. My girlfriends know what style I like. They know

To Viola,
e to do right, dare to be true,
You have a work that
no other can do.
Do it so kindly,
so bravely, so well,
That angels will hasten
the story to tell.

Your Friend, Annie
Haskinville, New York, February 08, 1890

Best Wishes

me by my style, and I recognize them by theirs.

Just like the clothes we wear, our lives have style, too. Each one of us is a unique creation. Let me offer some evidence from the world of fashion: If I try to wear an outfit that looks fabulous on someone else, I am usually disappointed that it doesn't work for me. And what looks good on me may not fit you at all. Each of us has been blessed with a one-of-a-kind combination of talents and abilities. We have been designed with much care and love. We have been made in the right fabric, the right color, and the right pattern, styled for only one form—mine for me and yours for you.

When we try to wear something that wasn't designed perfectly for us, the fit is never right. And when we try to be someone we're not, the fit is even more uncomfortable. Although I too easily get caught up in the world's opinion about fashion and style, I know that

Forget

TO MARY,
SHOULD WE BE
PARTED FAR AWAY,
YOU PERHAPS HEEDLESS
WHAT MAY BE MY LOT.
I WILL SEND YOU A
FLOWER AS A MESSENGER,
IT WILL WHISPER THIS,
FORGET-ME-NOT.

Your Truly, Charles Stuber
July 16, 1880

Me Not

Oh, you ca
the p
Of a littl

164 EAST 59TH STREET, N. Y.

my personal Designer has created only one me. I am the only one who wears that special and unique design. And the only applause I need to hear is from the Designer who created me and is proud of His work.

I think again of those dress-up clothes. They enabled me to be someone I wanted to be. But after I put them back in the box, I was still the same little girl. Our lives today parallel that common childhood experience. We can try to put on other clothes—other people's behaviors, attitudes, or actions—and make believe we are someone else. We can try to wear the suit that doesn't fit. But when the clothes are removed, we are still who we were designed to be.

I challenge you to discover your own unique pattern and wear it with style. Drape your life with joy, and appreciate the design that is the perfectly fashioned you. No one can pull it off like you can!

And, while you're at it, put on a scarf and add some pearls.

*Do not conform any longer to the pattern of this world, but be transformed by the renewing of your mind.*

*Romans 12:2*

Dreams of the
past
fill life
with delight.
*E. Nesbit.*

To Emma,

Our lives are songs,
and God writes the words,
As we set them to music at pleasure.
And our song grows glad or sweet or sad,
While we choose to fashion the measure.

But whether our lives are sad or not,
We give the world more pleasure.
And better ourselves if we set the words,
To some grand triumphant measure.

So we must write the song,
whatever the words,
And whatever the rhyme or meter;
And if it is sad, we should make it glad
Or if it is sweet, the sweeter.

*Respectfully, Jessie. 1883*

# CHAPTER FOUR

# NOT SETTLING FOR THE MERELY ACCEPTABLE
## To Be Worthy, Not Respectable

**M**ost women who were raised in the South own a string of pearls. Pearls have an established reputation in the halls of Southern living. They are worn to church, to weddings, and to dinner. They are always proper, appropriate for any occasion, including a quick run to the flea market. They go as well with an evening dress as they do with denim.

My husband bought me a string of genuine pearls for our twenty-fifth wedding anniversary. They are beautiful. But I don't wear them very often for fear of misplacing them. Instead I wear cultured pearls. If you look at my strands of pearls lying side by side, it is hard to distinguish the genuine from the imitation. Even experts cannot easily distinguish the difference. Both necklaces are beautiful, but the more valuable one is the strand of true pearls.

Cultured pearls are created when an irritant is inserted into a pearl oyster, forcing it to produce a commercially acceptable pearl. These pearls are not easy to distinguish from a genuine pearl even by an expert. The most common method of comparison is

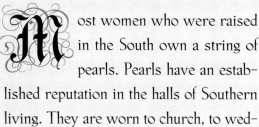

To Mattie,
Think truly and thy thought
Shall the world's famine feed.
Speak truly and thy word
Shall be a fruitful seed.
Live truly and thy life shall be
A great and noble creed.

From Bertha Stevens January 11, 1882

called "candling," a process that involves examining pearls in a strong light to confirm whether they are genuine.

The majority of the pearls sold today are either cultured or artificial, making the genuine pearl quite rare and very valuable. The term cultured pearls suggests that they are quality, but they nevertheless fall short of the genuine, the honest, and the true. They are less than they appear to be. They are respectable because we have deemed them acceptable. But being found worthy is something far greater than being found merely acceptable. After all, you'll never find the genuine and the artificial on the same silken string.

Many times when we need to be genuine, we allow ourselves to become like those cultured pearls. We try to live and act in a manner that is acceptable to those we want to impress. Although from the outside we appear to be real, we have allowed irritants—concerns about how we look and what people think of us—influence us and

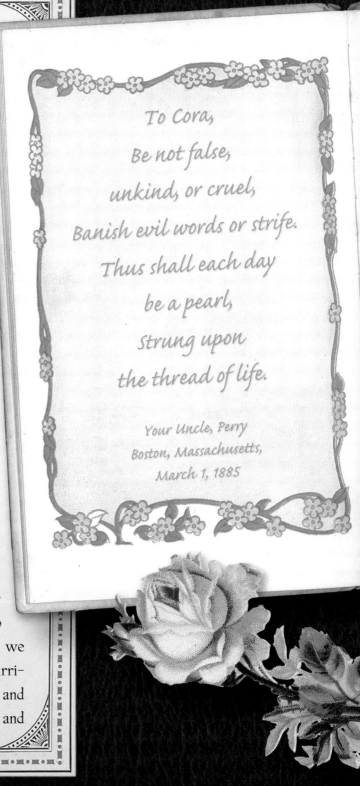

To Cora,
Be not false,
unkind, or cruel,
Banish evil words or strife.
Thus shall each day
be a pearl,
strung upon
the thread of life.

Your Uncle, Perry
Boston, Massachusetts,
March 1, 1885

DEAR BERTHA,
LOCK UP THY HEART,
KEEP SAFE THE KEY.
FORGET-ME-NOT,
TILL I DO THEE.

Your Friend, Emily Bartch
Silver Springs, Maryland, February 26, 1884

To Ida,

True worth is in being, not seeming;

In doing each day that goes by

Some little good, not in dreaming

Of great things to do by and by.

For whatever men do in their blindness

And in spite of the fancies of youth,

There is nothing so kingly as kindness

And nothing so royal as truth.

Your Friend, I. R. Woodward
Delta, Pennsylvania, June 18, 1889

Forget-me-not
Emblem of
True Love.

And we pray this in order
that you may live a life worthy
of the Lord and may please him
in every way: bearing fruit
in every good work [and] growing
in the knowledge of God.

Colossians 1:10

prompt us to produce an acceptable exterior. We have let ourselves be made to fit someone else's idea of perfection. We are respectable imitations of what is socially acceptable, and that may be quite different from what we need to be.

Our genuine worth comes from being true to God and true to whom He created us and calls us to be. It is to stand by a friend when all others won't. It is to stand up for our convictions and to live out our values. It is to, with an upward glance, acknowledge our need for love and acceptance—for God's love and acceptance, not man's. After all, as the Jeweler knows, being held up to the true light sets apart the pearl, separating the genuine from the common.

We are all pearls. Our worth is rooted in the One who created us, and it becomes apparent in the person we are when no one else can see us.

# CHAPTER FIVE

## KNOWING THE TRUE WEALTH OF FRIENDSHIP

### To Be Wealthy, Not Rich

I am very wealthy. I am wealthier than I ever dreamed or imagined I'd be. No, I didn't win the lottery, and I do live on a budget. My bank account is not very impressive, and the stockbroker doesn't consider me one of his most valued clients. But still I am wealthy beyond words.

My great wealth lies in treasure that cannot be bought with money or gold, treasure that is far more valuable than diamonds and rubies, treasure that is often sought after and seldom found. I'm talking about the treasure of devoted friendship.

My dear friend Linda is one of my richest treasures. We have been friends for almost forty years. Early in our friendship we shared clothes, had sleepovers every weekend, and were boy crazy together. We lived close to each other between ages eleven to sixteen, and the bond that resulted from those years has never been broken. Linda has lived in many different locations while I have remained fairly stationary. Despite the miles that separate us, when we get back together, it is as though time has stood still and we have never been apart. We are different in some of our views and tastes, but she's always there for me in sunshine and in shadows. She tells me the truth when I need to hear it, she lifts my spirits when I can't force a smile, and she loves me when I don't deserve it. And she knows I am there for her no matter what. I would be by her side if she needed me just as she

To Ella,

Friendship will weave a garland
Gold will link a chain
But love will form a clasp
Unbroken to remain.

From Minnie Doble
Manchester, New Hampshire, 1877

Best Wishes

True friendship is a golden chain
that links the happy years,
Each circle is a memory
that passing time endears.
I'm glad I have a cherished friend,
who's always grand and true,
Whose friendship means the world to me,
that cherished friend is you.

Love, Linda, 1973

Forget-
me-not

COUSIN REBECCA,
REMEMBER ME
WHEN YOU ARE HAPPY,
KEEP FOR ME ONE LITTLE SPOT.
IN THE DEPTHS OF THINE AFFECTION,
PLACE ONE SWEET FORGET-ME-NOT.

TO YOU AS A FRIEND, LILLIE RIGGLE
GOSHEN, INDIANA, 1882

To Mary,

Of all the gifts that Heaven bestows,

There's one above all measure,

And that's a friend; midst all our woes

A friend is found a treasure.

To thee I give that sacred name

For such thou art to me,

And ever proudly will I claim

To be a friend to thee.

*From Cora, 1881, Brooklyn, New York*

Greetings
My thoughts
are of you

would be for me. Although God has not allowed us to live close to each other for many years, we look forward to the day when we might again. But we know that even if that never happens on this earth, we will be together for eternity.

Linda and I have forged a chain made up of conversations and experiences, dreams and secrets, joys and sorrows, as we've shared our hearts and our lives, and love has formed the clasp. The links of this treasure and the clasp itself have been strengthened year after year by our devotion to each other. Long before I started my sentiment album collection, Linda gave me a beautiful book entitled Words of Life. When I started writing this book, I came across an inscription she had left for me.

Tears come to my eyes as I read these beautiful lines. Written to me when we were both young women with many years ahead of us, these priceless words still enrich my soul. They are a treasure that riches could never buy.

As if Linda's precious friendship weren't wealth enough, I have been blessed with even more. Friends who truly love me. Friends who pray with me and for me. Friends who stand by my side when I am in need. Yet much of the wealth that enriches my life comes when I have had the privilege of passing on to others the kind of devoted friendship that people have extended to me. I am richly blessed when I am able to offer the grace of devoted friendship to others.

One of my most valued possessions is a beautifully crafted and carefully decorated treasure box. In that box I keep cards and letters filled with encouraging words and sincere thoughts that I've received from precious friends throughout the years. At times, I read these tokens of love, and their words are a taste of heaven in my heart. The contents of that box are of infinite worth to me. I know that if my home caught on fire, I would not reach for the financial documents first. I would instead make sure that my treasure box was safe, for that is where evidence of my true wealth lies.

*has chosen you...*
*to be His people,*
*His treasured*
*possession.*

*Deuteronomy 7:6*

# CHAPTER SIX
# FOLLOWING GOD'S PATTERN FOR OUR LIVES
## To Study Hard

Decorating is a passion of mine. I eagerly await the next issue of my decorating magazine the way some folks anticipate Christmas morning. I study each issue and have files filled with pictures of beautiful homes, studies of decorating techniques, and how-tos for every new trick of the trade. I never knew that every room needs a splash of black until I learned that it adds a bit of richness. Now there is a touch of black in all of my rooms, and it works more than I could have imagined.

I love to learn about different decorating styles. I haven't completely decided which is my favorite so I blend them all. I decorate with as much soul as I can muster. I find it a challenge to use any old object in a way it was never designed to be used, and I've bought all these fun items on a budget. My style could be labeled "early depression eclectic thrift shop"! It works

for me—and it keeps my friends wondering!

I just converted my son's abandoned bedroom into my personal study. It has a lady's antique writing desk, a breakfront that displays my autograph book collection, and, of course, a black needlepoint pillow. It's my room. Just as our words and actions are reflections of our hearts, my little room is a reflection of me. You can see my personality in it. It's my study—and it's a study of me.

Needlepoint intrigues me. I have needlepoint pictures and pillows in every room of my home. They represent someone's careful work, patient stitching, and generous gift of time. They are not only beautiful to look upon, but each one also suggests a story. They also point to the storyteller, the

To Gracie,
If you would have
your learning stay,
Be patient,
don't learn too fast.
The man who travels
a mile each day
Will get 'round
the world at last.

Your Friend, Lizzie A. Main
Rochester, New Hampshire
December 31, 1885

6250/4

artist who made something beautiful with a needle and some thread. Once just a pattern stamped on a blank canvas, the design has come alive with colorful threads and well-placed stitches. After the design was completed, the background was filled in with a neutral color, providing an effective contrast for the artist's work.

Just like a needlepoint design, you and I can also easily fade into the background of our lives and miss what we could have been. The better choice is to study God's Word and then pattern our lives for a sweeter purpose, filling each day with beauty and style. It can be tedious work, becoming the best we can be, making sure each stitch is in the proper place, part of God's unique and perfect pattern for us and the product of our mutual labor with God's love.

The underside of a needlepoint is not nearly so lovely as the front. Hidden away from sight are broken threads,

FORGET ME NOT

To Miss Annie.
I thought and thought in vain.
And then I thought ag[...]
I'd write in this lonely spot.
The words forget-me-n[...]

From Mabel---Melrose. Maryland. January 6. 1888[...]

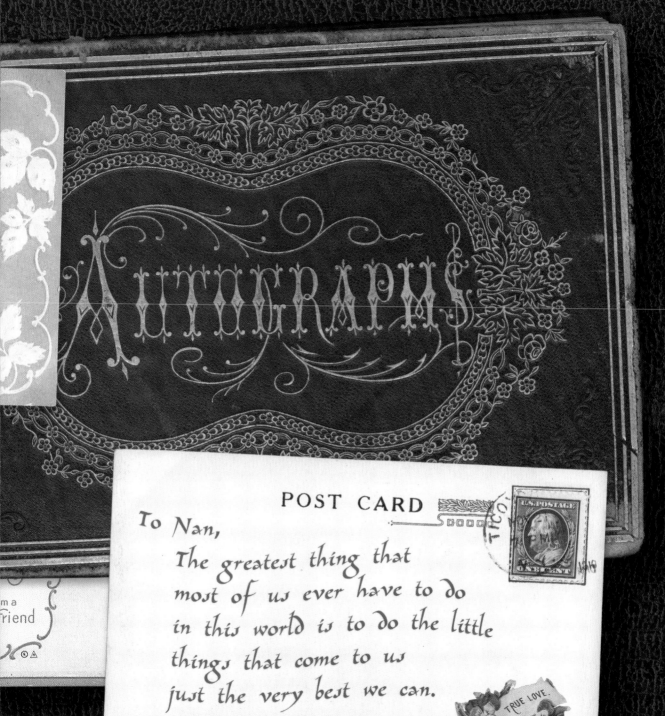

POST CARD

To Nan,
The greatest thing that most of us ever have to do in this world is to do the little things that come to us just the very best we can.

Love, Your Friend,
Frances

TRUE LOVE.

To Georgia,
Our lives are
a golden knot,
tied by
an angel's hand.
I hope yours
is tied so tight,
that it will
forever stand.

Your Friend, Albert Cross
Harney City, Oregon
March 17, 1909

Returns.

haphazard knots, and tangled colors. When we look beneath a canvas, we can more fully appreciate the beauty of its finished side. Much like a needlepoint, similar evidence of labor and love can always be found in our lives, often hidden from view but occasionally appearing as a thread of disappointment or a knot of broken dreams. These threads, knots, and tangles—perhaps known only to us—help us more fully appreciate the beauty of the other side.

Before time, God stamped our lives with a pattern. He has blessed us with colorful threads and perfect directions. Each day that we study His ways, follow His directions, and stay within the pattern outlined for us, we add stitches that will bring the pattern to life. The real beauty will be seen in the finished design.

We are God's workmanship.

Ephesians 2:10

# CHAPTER SEVEN

## HAVING A HUMBLE AND COMPASSIONATE HEART

### To Think Quietly, Talk Gently, Act Frankly

By the world's standards, my father was considered a short man. Today he might be labeled "vertically challenged," but he described himself as a tall man in disguise. Although physically short in stature, he stood tall spiritually. He truly was a man who thought quietly, spoke gently, and acted frankly.

With little support from his family and no money, my father was a self-made man. Highly intelligent and motivated, he pursued his dreams. He worked hard for all that he achieved, never complaining about the cost. As a respected physicist, he acquired several government patents for his work. I can remember cleaning up after evening meals and finding Daddy's napkin covered with very interesting mathematical equations. I only wish I had saved them!

My father also proved his courage when he served his country aboard the USS Indiana during World War II, before I was born. But he could not have been more courageous than when he suffered through an illness that would end his life too early. He was a well-respected man among men, and I was always proud to be his daughter. I admire him for many reasons, but perhaps the most outstanding in my memory is the tender compassion that he showed others and his genuinely humble heart.

The needs my father had known in his own

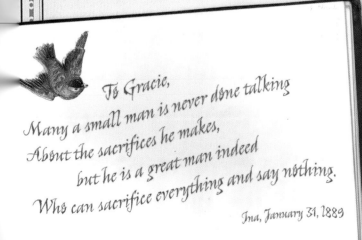

To Gracie,

Many a small man is never done talking
About the sacrifices he makes,
but he is a great man indeed
Who can sacrifice everything and say nothing.

Ina, January 31, 1889

MANY HAPPY RETURNS OF TH[E]

DESIGN COPYRIGHTED JOHN WINSCH, 1912.

1992

To Lizzie,
Live for those who love you
    For those whose hearts are true;
For the heaven
    that smiles above you
And the good
    that you may do.

Your Friend, Lou
Cordova, Illinois, 1885

Forget

Dear Anna,

You ask for your album a rhyme.
With pleasure I hear and obey.
Refusal were folly or crime.
For who could to say nay.
Forget-me-not, forget-me-never,
Until we meet in Heaven together.

From MaryAnn Lacke. 1887

Me Not

Best Wishes

life made him more sensitive to those around him who were in need. He would deliver groceries to a doorstep or quietly pay someone's electric bill. He would give an extra offering at church to help meet an emergency request, and he always had a kind word for a wounded spirit. His compassion ran deep.

But I found the humility of my father's heart even more noteworthy than his many generous acts of compassion. True to his nature, he didn't want his kindness to be acknowledged by man. He did not look for his reward on earth; he stored up his treasure in heaven. He thought quietly concerning a need, spoke gently to the Lord in prayer about that need, and then acted to relieve the need. Countless lives were blessed as he silently taught that truly loving compassion always acts in partnership with a quiet, humble spirit.

I look at my sons today and see my father in them. Both are young men of compassionate hearts and humble spirits. My prayer is that they will live out their grandfather's legacy, understanding that a life of compassion and humility brings its own rewards.

"I have fought the fight, I have finished the race" is the inscription engraved on my father's headstone. These words are a testimony to his perseverance, another of the character traits that shaped his life. My dad was a gentle giant who quietly left some remarkable footprints. When his life's journey was over, it was easy to see where he had been.

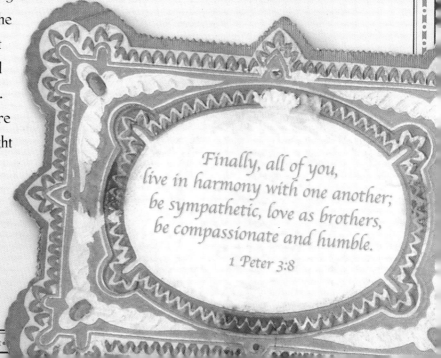

*Finally, all of you, live in harmony with one another; be sympathetic, love as brothers, be compassionate and humble.*

1 Peter 3:8

# CHAPTER EIGHT

## LEARNING TO LISTEN WITH ONE'S HEART

### To Listen to Stars and Birds, and Babes and Sages with Open Heart

Life has its many mysteries, and certain matters will never be explained. My sister Melanie and I have pondered some of these bewilderments for many years. We wonder, for instance, how our children can hear us whisper something we don't want them to hear but sometimes not hear us when we're speaking directly to them. We wonder why our husbands never heard the loud crying of our infant children when it bolted us out of bed. And why do our husbands always have to play a video in ultraloud surround sound? And why can't they hear themselves snoring? Melanie and I have not been very scientific in our pursuit of answers, but we have concluded that our husbands and our children are selective listeners. And we've realized that there's a big difference between truly listening and merely hearing.

Think about it. We can hear but not really listen. We can hear with our ears but not with our hearts.

In our high-tech world, we can be surrounded by sound twenty-four hours a day. We can so saturate our lives with noise that it can become impossible for us to really listen for and hear what really matters. If we aren't careful, the noise of modern life can overwhelm us, deafening us to all that is important.

I live in a surround-sound suburban

To Mattie,

Flowers themselves whatever their hue,
With all their fragrance
and all their glistening,
Call to the heart for inward listening.

Nan Pierce
Ashtabula, Ohio, 1882

Faithful and true.

neighborhood. My neighbors live an arm's length away, and the noise of suburban life is ever present. After living here for so long, I have become conditioned to the constant activity. My heart has silenced the surround sound, now accustomed to its presence. Although the noise is always there, I no longer pay attention to it. But when I travel to the mountains of North Carolina, I experience a different kind of surround sound. There I find the quiet sounds of nature. I hear the birds that sing and the wind that blows through the trees. I hear it because my open heart has been stilled to listen.

Oh, birds live in my suburban neighborhood. They have always been there, but I don't hear them for all the noise. I have not trained my heart to listen to their song there.

I want to recondition my heart to tranquility so I can listen to what I am hearing in the everyday. I want to practice the art of stillness because life's

Place
Stamp here

Domestic
one cent

Foreign
two cents

Harper
...nroe St.
...hburg
Va

U.S. POSTAGE
1 CENT

EVERIES

Forget-
-me-not

Friend Mildred,
You call this book a garden plot,
To fill with friendship flowers.
I only plant forget-me-nots,
To bloom among its bowers.

Yours Truly, Katy Martin
March 18, 1902

...etings
...From a
...r Friend

To Rebecca,

Now doth the little busy bee

Improve each shining hour

And gather honey all the day

From every opening flower.

Hazell Dell Whitacre,
Nine Years Old
January 20, 1900

C.G.R.

Listen to advice
and accept instruction,
and in the end you will be wise.

Proverbs 19:20

distractions often change my focus from truly listening to merely hearing. Setting aside a time each morning to quiet my heart and to listen to what I am hearing gives me great peace. Pulling away from the distractions in life and focusing on being still has become a cherished time for me. It is a time that teaches me to listen with an open heart.

And we can receive so many valuable lessons when we listen. There is the innocence of a young child's questions and the wisdom of an older saint's counsel. There is the beauty that the stars speak forth and the uplifting melodies of a bird's gentle song. With so much to hear, we must carefully select what we listen to and choose what will edify our souls. If we draw apart from all the noise that fills our world and quiet our open hearts, we will be able to listen to the blessed voice of God.

# CHAPTER NINE

# LOOKING FOR HEAVEN'S SUNSHINE
## To Bear All Cheerfully

I am married to a morning person. My sweet husband wakes up quickly, takes a morning run, and whistles in the shower. Enough said.

I, on the other hand, am not now nor have I ever been a morning person. It is not my nature to wake up cheerfully, and my idea of an early riser is a breakfast tray in bed around 8 a.m. I decide what I think about the day an hour after I shower. Then, depending on the traffic and the humidity, I choose to bear all cheerfully, or I choose to just bear it. And my actions will be determined by my choice of attitudes. At the moment I'm smiling. We'll wait and see about the rest of the morning.

My friend Shirley teaches me a lot. Older and wiser than I, she has mentored me in Shirley's School of Attitude. If I whine about a task, Shirley will say in her sweet South Carolina drawl, "Don't make me get harsh with you. You know you can do this." She never lets me get away with a negative attitude. Her father died when she was a young girl, so she learned from her mother the art of optimism. "You just do what you have to do" is her motto.

I have never seen Shirley get discouraged or upset about anything. She can cheerfully entertain a very large group on short notice, and she actually enjoys cooking all day. She is an extraordinary hostess, who makes everyone feel comfortable and relaxed. She has all the grace of a lovely Southern belle and the pizzazz of a firecracker. I love to be with her not only because she is fun,

To Maggie,

Be we rich or be we poor,
There are trials to endure.
Be we high or be we low,
There are pleasures
that bestow

On our lives a luster sweet
Every time the shadows meet
Sunshine can the
shadows fright,
Smiles can make
the darkness bright.

Your Friend, L. M. Dice
Boiling Springs Primary School
February 08, 1882

3345/5.

That you'll

but also because her positive, upbeat attitude is contagious. She chooses to be cheerful in all circumstances, and she teaches me by her example.

We will all face some adversity in our lifetimes. We may walk through the valleys of pain or discouragement; we may have to overcome fear of failure or financial setback; or we may face the loss of friends or family members to serious illness. But even in those valleys, we can still find sunshine. Sometimes a cloud can hide it, but eventually the sun does come back out. Heaven's sunshine is always available to those who choose it.

Recently, my heart was touched by heaven's sunshine. A couple I know offers a remarkable example of bearing all cheerfully. Totally committed to each other and to the Lord, this husband and wife walked through an extremely difficult valley together.

There is no flower growin In any garden plot,

TO COUSIN CORA,
WHEN THINGS DON'T GO
TO SUIT YOU
AND THE WORLD SEEMS
UPSIDE DOWN,
DON'T WASTE YOUR TIME
IN FRETTING
BUT DRIVE AWAY THE FROWN.

FROM EVA KRUM
FLOWERFIELD, MICHIGAN, OCTOBER 14, 1889

To Candace,

Forget-me-not,
Forget-me-never,
Until we meet,
In heaven together.

From Your Loving Mother, Belinda

January 12, 1885

To Millie,
There are hours
the heart grows weary,
All life's joys seem torn away,
Pass them, note
the bright hours only.
Catch life's sunshine
while you may.

From Agnes Hoagland
March 30, 1883

THIS SIDE FO

Hello Tw
this fin
and as h
Havie a
down a
to stay y
see Read
how on
he call
nomen
at an
with
colic

Duclos    123 MAIN ST. NASHUA, N.H.

ST CARD.

U.S. POSTAGE

Let us not get tired
of doing what is right,
for after a while we will
reap a harvest of blessing
if we don't get discouraged
and give up.

Galatians 6:9, TLB

She was diagnosed with a cancer that would eventually take her life. Undaunted by the illness, the two of them maintained a positive attitude. At her funeral service, the source of their strength became more apparent. We learned that, every morning when they would awaken, she would look over at her husband, not knowing what the day would bring, and say, "Honey, are you ready for some heavenly sunshine today?"

Both the husband and wife truly believed that we should not just bear all that comes our way, but bear it all cheerfully. They not only believed it; they chose to live it. Now that she is in perfect peace, her husband can smile because he knows that his precious wife is enjoying some very real heavenly sunshine.

# Chapter Ten

# Admiring a Mother's Courage
## To Do All Bravely

My mother and father were childhood sweethearts. Mother never dated or loved anyone else. She fell madly in love with him when she was fifteen, married him when she was eighteen, and gave birth to me when she was nineteen. Mother raised five children (she actually wanted eight!). We never missed a meal, a doctor's appointment, or a Little League baseball game. We always had clean clothes in our dressers and toothpaste in the bathroom. Now she is a wonderful and beloved grandmother of thirteen and is affectionately known to many as "Mama Jean." She remembers all the family birthdays, and she makes sure no one in the family is overlooked at Christmas.

Besides running a home, she volunteered in every one of her children's many activities. Room mother, Girl Scout helper, team mom—the list goes on and on. Despite everything she did for us, she still found some time to win several ribbons in flower arranging competitions. She taught Sunday school for over forty years with us by her side; she always decorated the church for special occasions; and she has coordinated many, many weddings.

We did not grow up in an affluent home. Daddy's paycheck was distributed

Dear Emma,
One by one thy duties wait thee.
Let thy whole strength go to each.
Let no future dreams elate thee.
Learn those first what these can teach.
Every hour that fleets so slowly.
Has its task to do or bear.
Luminous the crown.
And holy when each gem is set with care.

Affectionately, Your Mother, 1883

Forget-me-not

to the various envelopes my mom used to budget the household money. In the event of an emergency, she would shift money from one envelope to another. It was not a high-tech system, but it worked—and I was amazed by how she managed to make that paycheck stretch. She sewed my clothes and always made sure that the family wore matching colors at Easter. Hardly ever buying anything new for herself, she became a very good thrift shop customer. To this day, she still knows how to make secondhand work beautifully.

Mom did not go to college, but she has earned a doctorate degree in the school of life. She devoted her life to nurturing our family, and my father devoted his life to supporting our family. He and Mom were making plans to retire and enjoy the fruits of their hard labor, but life can be harsh—those plans were never to be realized. Dad's life was cut short by a tragic illness.

*Forget*

To Friend Anna,
When days are dark
and friends are few,
Remember me and I will you.
May every blessing be your lot,
I only ask—forget-me-not.

Your Friend, Mary Siebers
July 22, 1883

*Me Not*

FORGET ME NOT

HERE'S GLADNESS
IN
REMEMBRANCE

To the sessions of sweet silent thought,
Summon up remembrance of things past.
*Shakespeare.*

To Sarah,
you may break,
you may shatter
the vase
if you will,
but the scent
of the roses
will cling
around it still

From Annie
February 19, 1882

Her children arise and call
her blessed; her husband also,
and he praises her:
"Many women do noble things,
but you surpass them all."
Charm is deceptive,
and beauty is fleeting;
but a woman who fears
the LORD is to be praised.
Give her the reward
she has earned, and let
her works bring her praise
at the city gate.

*Proverbs 31:28–31*

When he died, Mother had to continue on alone. Suddenly a young widow, she faced an uncertain future and broken dreams. Bitterness and discouragement knocked on her heart's door for years. Though she still occasionally opens that door, it doesn't stay open for long.

Mom has a family and friends who need her, and she rises to the occasion even when the pain rages inside her heart. She did not ask for the job, but she is now the head of the family. And though hers continues to be a difficult journey, she faithfully moves forward. She still has lonely days and questions for God that can't be answered here on earth. But Mom has chosen to use her experiences to nurture and minister to other widows, encouraging them to move forward in spite of the obstacles. She has learned that life is not always fair, but it marches on nevertheless. She has chosen "to do all bravely."

I LOVE YOU, MOM.

# CHAPTER ELEVEN
## SLOWING DOWN AND SAVORING THE BLESSINGS
### To Await Occasions and Hurry Never

I sometimes wish life were an endless tea party. I just love having people over for tea. And it's not just the tiny sandwiches, tasty scones, and delectable pastries that make having tea so inviting. It's the time that must be set aside to enjoy it. After all, a "proper" tea is orderly and structured. The sandwiches are served first, the scones second, and the pastries last. The warm tea has to be sipped so that the flavor can be savored. We must take the time to open our hearts to joy and relaxation. Our modern, fast-paced world is satisfied with an instant teabag, but our spirit longs for something much finer. The special ritual of tea invites us to slow down, wait for the next course, and truly enjoy the company of our guests. It takes more time to measure out the loose leaves and let them steep, but the flavor is worth the wait.

My father always encouraged me not to wish my life away, but I didn't listen. When I was a young girl, all I wanted was to be sixteen. But then, I couldn't enjoy being sixteen because I wanted to be twenty-one. Then, after twenty-one, I wanted to be married. After the wedding, I immediately wanted to be a mother. God was in February while I was in June. Never fully enjoying the moment I was living in, I tried to push God to move me forward in time. I have missed much of the blessing in my life because I was too anxious to experience the future. Now, I appreciate how wise my father was.

Just as we are invited to enjoy each course at teatime, we are given the opportunity to savor each phase of life's

The images
long forsaken.

*Heine.*

To Hannah,

One step and then another
and the longest walk is ended,
One stitch and then another
and the longest rent is mended.
One flake and then another
and the deepest drift is laid,
One brick and then another
and the highest wall is made.
Though life be filled with crosses,
they are given one by one,
And when the last one passes
we'll shout the victory won.
Then listen to the Master
and hear Him say, "Well done."
And then through endless ages
the anthem still shall swell
Of Him who ever liveth,
"He doeth all things well."
Toil on then, faithful worker,
for others your life will see,
He'll say when the work is finished,
"Ye did it unto me."

From Alexandria, 1900

journey. But sometimes in our haste to get to the next stage, we fail to enjoy the present one. I went to college, married my husband, and soon had my first child. Motherhood was wonderful, but hard. I loved being a young mom, but the job was relentless. At times the monotony of the everyday chores was overwhelming. Then, before I knew it, my boys had graduated from college, and my life had changed radically. It seemed that, in the blink of an eye, I had an empty nest. Still, instead of living in the moment and relishing each day, I continued to run ahead of God looking for what was next. I can only wonder how many blessings eluded my restless heart.

We live in a world where time is a precious commodity. It is so valuable because we never seem to have enough of it. We have such busy schedules that we barely seem to enjoy our pursuits. And often we are

To Ella,
Live today!
Tomorrow never yet
on any human being
rose or set.

Truly Your Friend, Edwin
South Cornish, New Hampshire, July

Autographs.

Forget

To Debbie,
Remember me
and let's have tea.
Drink it hot and
forget-me-not.

Love, April
1895

me not

## POST CARD

U.S. POSTAGE

To Dollie,

    May He who painted each floweret fair,
    And guides the lone bird through the pathless air
    Mete out to thee each day and each hour,
    With infinite love and infinite power.

From Annie Fox
Brooklyn, New York
June 21, 1878

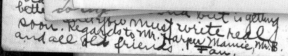

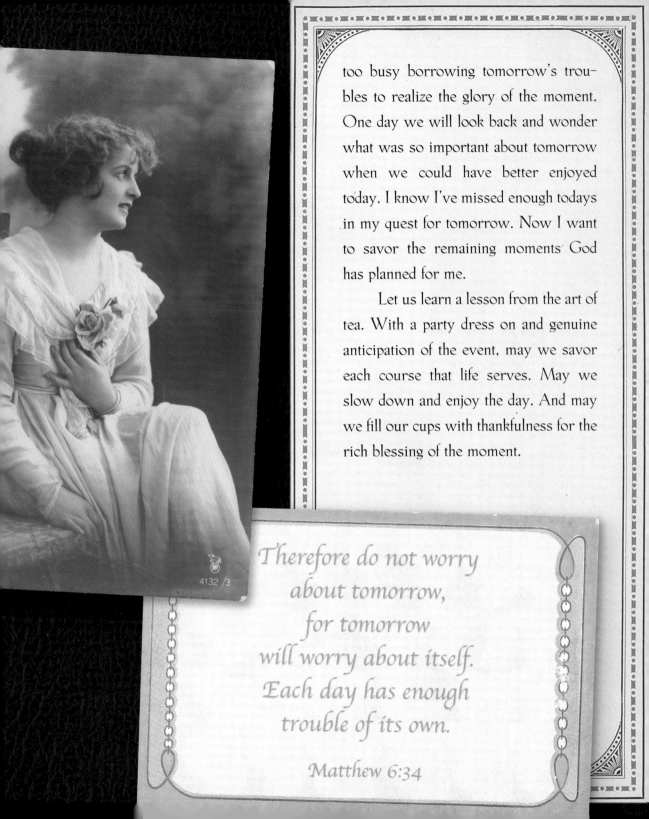

too busy borrowing tomorrow's troubles to realize the glory of the moment. One day we will look back and wonder what was so important about tomorrow when we could have better enjoyed today. I know I've missed enough todays in my quest for tomorrow. Now I want to savor the remaining moments God has planned for me.

Let us learn a lesson from the art of tea. With a party dress on and genuine anticipation of the event, may we savor each course that life serves. May we slow down and enjoy the day. And may we fill our cups with thankfulness for the rich blessing of the moment.

Therefore do not worry
about tomorrow,
for tomorrow
will worry about itself.
Each day has enough
trouble of its own.

Matthew 6:34

# CHAPTER TWELVE

## WONDERING AT THE MIRACLES IN EVERY DAY

### To Let the Spiritual Unbidden and Unconscious Grow up through the Common

I am a dog lover. I have always wanted to have a large number of dogs, but since I don't live in the country, I know I can't. But I do have three dogs, and they are wonderful friends. They always love you, and they never say anything bad about you. Our dogs are a part of our family. We include them in the family Christmas picture, and we take them on family vacations.

When my boys were ready to leave for college, they surprised me with a Christmas present that you can't return. Macon was the most precious little puppy I had ever seen, and I fell in love with her at first sight. (I also fell over her and broke my foot, but that's another story.) From the very beginning, she slept in the bed with me and followed me around all day. When I was sick, she would lie by my side. When I was happy, she would wag her tail. She was the closest thing to a daughter I would ever have. It left a huge hole in my heart when I lost her to an illness. I will never forget her and the lessons about life that she left with me.

Consider, for instance, that a dog's life is made up of three simple elements. They eat, they sleep, and they play, preferably outdoors. Macon viewed the outdoors with wonder and excitement. She was a real "tomdog." She would run around, chasing insects and lizards. And she could see what I couldn't. I would look at a flower garden and see only flowers, but Macon would look at the same garden and see every inch as worthy of careful exploration. She would disappear into the hedge and emerge a moment later with a ball that had been hidden for years. Where I had seen only a garden, she saw a treasure. How many times do you and I walk through life and miss the treasures that lie unnoticed along our path?

Our society thrives on constant activity. We are told that we

Many Happy
Returns of the Day

Forget

Dear Anna,
Remember me,
    When these lines you see.
Although you see me not,
    Let others say whatever they may,
    But oh, forget-me-not.

Yours Truly,
Annie Brenken, 1884

Me Not

must be busy in order to be valuable. The busier we are, the better we are. We need to do three things at once to be considered productive. We plan our time as if we had thirty-six-hour days and forty-five-day months. In this quest for success as the world defines it, we often miss the blessings along the paths of our journey. It is the journey itself that should bring fulfillment and satisfaction.

Every morning, we are given an opportunity to find the miracle in that new day. Often, without realizing it, we pass by beauty because we are preoccupied with the common. As we limit our vision to the items on our to-do list, we miss the wonder that exists along our path. Splendor is all around us; we just need to put on different glasses.

I never believed those who told me that my eyesight would change after I turned forty. But now I have a pair of reading glasses in every room of the house. My purse looks like an optical store. I always took it for granted that I would have twenty-twenty vision forever, but now glasses have become part of my world.

But those glasses help me with just one kind of vision. There's another

To Nellie,
Walk in the light
and thou shalt see
Thy path,
though thorny, bright;
For God by grace
shall dwell in thee
And God Himself is light.

From C. A. Freeman
Hartford, Connecticut
May 7, 1877

## To Dollie.

Enjoy today the flowers that blow
Even though they fade amid their blowing:

Enough for you to calmly know
That God has other flowers in growing,

As fair as those so swiftly going
Enjoy today the flowers that blow
Though you to fade amid their blowing:

Enough for you to calmly know
That God has other gardens growing,
And you to fairer blooms are going.

From Lavinia Williams
August 25, 1885

REMEMBRANCE

embrance," says my token,
no words my lips may say,
u hear them softly spoken
heart to yours to-day.

To Belle,

May your path be strewn,
With roses of love.
And your anchor be cast,
In the heavens above.

Your Friend, Josie, 1879

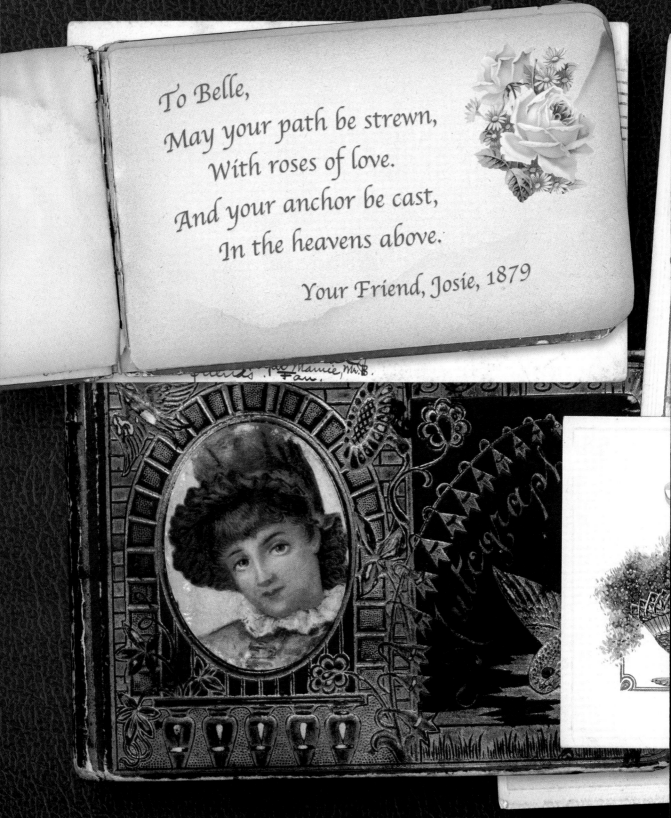

"You have made known to me the paths of life; you will fill me with joy in your presence."

Acts 2:28

important kind of vision I've needed to fine-tune. I've realized that I never had twenty-twenty vision for what matters most in life. Oh, I've thought I was seeing everything clearly, but you and I need to see everything better than we do. And we need to see things we've never seen before. We need to put on glasses so that our vision will become clearer. There are miracles and blessings all around us that we may never see unless we are willing to put these glasses on. When our vision is perfected and more focused, we will stand in amazement at the wonder and awe that surround us. And we will walk our journey with eyes fixed upon the path, finally able to see the majesty and the mystery, the blessing and the beauty, that rise up from the common.

As she helped me learn to look for hidden treasures, Macon opened my eyes to the adventure and wonder of life. She wasn't given a long life, but her life was one of constant adventure. She walked through each new day with new fascination. I admired her journey, for she taught me to see with wonder and find the miracle in everything common.

# CHAPTER THIRTEEN

## BEING TUNED FOR THE MUSIC OF LIFE

### This Is to Be My Symphony

I love classical music. I marvel at the intricate sounds created by the different instruments. Each plays its own song, and those songs, distinctive and lovely when played alone, create a magnificent sound when they come together. Beautiful music, designed specifically for each unique and perfectly tuned instrument, is blended together in a delightfully harmonious symphony as each musician follows the conductor's lead.

I want every day of my life to be that kind of symphony. I want my heart to be in harmony with a song from the Lord so that I may please others with the music of my life. I want to have both the dedication it takes to practice daily and the willingness to make sacrifices for those who will benefit from my song. I must be willing to be tuned, remembering that it is a daily necessity. I must be willing to play the score that has been written just for me, knowing that

each note I play contributes to the symphony. And, most importantly, I need to follow the lead of the Conductor. I want my symphony to be pleasing to His ears, for He has written the music that I play.

To close this book, I leave with you a symphony of words written in 1854 from one friend to another. These words, like those I've found in every album I own, invite us to share in the lives of both the woman who wrote them and the one who received them. And though

# Forget-me-not

To Dollie.

Think that I will forget thee? No!

Hush the voice that tells thee so,

Other friends may be forgot,

But still will I forget-thee-not.

your friend, Celia, September 18, 1878

Hello Twee

this fin

and as b

Winter

these women traveled the journey of life before you and I did, I feel a real sense of connection to them and to the thoughts of their hearts. Their words call us to forget them not. So, let us honor their lives by continuing in their path. Though times have certainly changed, the hearts of women clearly seem to have remained the same. Friendship, love, truth, devotion, honor, family, and faith will always be important to the human soul. It is my prayer that you may know those things that they so treasured.

Likewise, I wish you beauty, riches, and honor—but most of all, I pray that your heart knows the treasure of the One who loves you eternally.

"For God so loved the world that he gave his one and only Son, that whoever believes in him shall not perish but have eternal life."

John 3:16

To Martha,

I have taken my pen, my friend, to write a line upon these pages, where so many friends have inscribed their names and recorded their wishes. And what shall I wish for you? Shall I wish for you beauty? 'Tis fleeting as the summer cloud, even as the morning cloud, and early dew, which soon pass away. Shall I wish for you riches? They perish with the using. They take to themselves wings and fly away. "The moth and rust corrupt and thieves of time break through and steal." Shall it be honor, which I shall desire for you? It does not promise happiness. Shall I wish for you friends? True it is but for friends and friendship, this world would be a dreary place. But friends and friendship too often are but names. There are exceptions, it is true, and many, but the truest friends may die, and those best loved and trusted are often taken first. Truly—beauty, riches, honor, friends, like all things earthly, are fleeting and transitory. They endure but for a season and they are gone.

And yet I do wish for you beauty, not of face and form merely, but the beauty of those that are arrayed in the robe of Christ's righteousness, and adorned with the graces of His spirit. I would wish for you riches—not the riches of this world, but an inheritance among the saints in light even an inheritance incorruptible and that fadeth not away—a crown of glory, of honor, and immortality. I would also wish for you honor, but it is the honor that belongs to those who are the sons of God, the "heirs of glory"—such honor will indeed bring happiness. And friends, may they ever be yours—kind and true, the same ever, in sickness or in health, in prosperous or adverse circumstances—but not only earthly friends—may He who is the sinners' friend be yours. May He who loves all who put their trust in Him, be the chosen friend of your heart, and may you ever share His friendship, which shall last for all eternity.

May such beauty—such riches—such honor—and such a friend, be yours, now and forever.

From Mary, 1854

Forget-
me-
Not